C000142149

BYGONE DAYS
DOVEDALE AND THE
MANIFOLD VALLEY

Lindsey Porter

ASHBOURNE EDITIONS

Published by:
Ashbourne Editions
12 Compton, Ashbourne, Derbyshire DE6 1DA
Tel: 01335 347349   Fax: 01335 347303

British Library Cataloguing in Publishing Data:
A catalogue record for this book is available from the British Library

ISBN 1 873775 15 6

Frontispiece:
Ladies at a stall, Stepping Stones, Dovedale

Cover illustration:
AD Beresford, Underhill, Longnor, Buxton

Printed in Great Britain by J W Arrowsmith Ltd, Bristol

INTRODUCTION

Dovedale and the Manifold Valley have been popular visitor attractions ever since the railway to Ashbourne made the area more accessible. The extension of the line to Buxton in 1890 was a relative late comer, bringing railway stations to isolated communities such as Tissington, Alsop-en-le-Dale and Hartington. It was followed in 1904 by the Leek and Manifold Light Railway. This was virtually sixty years after the railway had reached Leek and Ashbourne, which had enabled people from the cities such as The Potteries and Derby to make inexpensive excursions to the area, although many people from the former also went to Rudyard Lake and Alton Towers.

Even before the coming of the railway, people would walk or hitch a lift on anything with wheels to get to the events such as Tissington Well Dressing or Newhaven Fair. So far as the valleys were concerned, it was Dovedale, especially round where the Stepping Stones are now located, which was the most popular. Much of the Manifold and the Hamps valleys were inaccessible as there was no footpath running down these valleys. Only after the Manifold Railway closed in 1934 did this situation change. The valleys were much less wooded than they are now, principally because of a reduction in grazing by cattle and sheep. The photographs in this book show how much woodland has extended compared to a century ago.

This collection of photographs draws together images of life in and around the valleys up to some thirty years ago. While some of them have been published previously, many have not and some, such as the remains of Crowdecote and Milldale Mills, the Ecton Creamery and Swainsley Tunnel photos are probably unique. This is the first time that a book of old photographs of these two popular valleys has been published. They bring together Victorian scenes of Dovedale; places of work, such as Ecton Mines in 1883 and the Hartington and Ecton cheese factories; the travelling horse-drawn shop in Longnor; the interior of Ilam Hall when it was a private house owned by the Hanbury's and much more. Several photographs record properties which do not survive. They include the formal part of Ilam Hall; Hartington's penny lodging house; stations at Ashbourne, Parsley Hay, Tissington and on the Manifold line; the Ilam Rock tea-room; the mill at Mill Dale, etc.

Collectively, they help create an idea of how the area used to be in days gone by. I hope you enjoy them.

Several photographs were kindly lent to me and I wish to acknowledge the assistance I have received from the National Trust, Bill Bailey, Jean and Peter Bailey, Mary Winstone, David Gordon, Alan Salt, Shirley Taylor, and PL Wilson.

DOVEDALE

The entrance to Dovedale. Looking towards the Stepping Stones from near the footbridge upriver from the car park, with Thorpe Cloud rising on the right (above)

The river immediately below where the Stepping Stones are now situated (below)

Old photographs of Dovedale are particularly fascinating as they allow us to see how the valley has changed over the years. There has been a substantial increase in tree and scrub cover. A few years ago, the National Trust took a chain saw into the valley and received a lot of criticism. This was misguided, for the Trust removed a lot of invasive sycamore and unwanted scrub, opening up views of rock features enjoyed in Victorian times. A major reason why the hawthorn and extra trees have flourished has been a reduction in sheep grazing. Although the valley is famous for its relict ash woods, it is probable that these only survived around the more inaccessible cliffs, the rest of the woodland being relatively recent in date

Also relatively recent are the stepping stones at Thorpe Cloud, as they do not appear on some Victorian photographs, (below). They did exist in 1875 however. Comparing this scene with today, the whole of the west (Staffordshire) bank is now well wooded and trees now line the river bank in places

The Stepping Stones area has always been very popular although it was more commonly reached from Thorpe via Lin Dale. There used to be stalls by the river and donkey rides. The path started adjacent to the Peveril of the Peak Hotel (above). The notice to the left of the drive entrance reads 'Direct to the Dale'

The lower scene shows the bottom of Lin Dale with some of the stalls and the donkeys (which came daily from Ashbourne)

Two views of the donkeys fording the river

Another group of visitors crossing the Dove

Sheep rounded up on the Staffordshire bank, near to where the Stepping Stones are now, possibly for dipping (above)

The lower photograph shows the gate behind the sheep on the above picture. In the middle distance the first of the tors may be seen — known as Dovedale Castle

The mass tourism to Dovedale, is no recent feature, as this scene shows. The photograph was taken in the late 1950's

Dovedale Castle

Dovedale Church, opposite the pump house near to Tissington Spires

Tissington Spires (above)

The upstream side of the Lion Head Rock (below)

The Straits (previously known as the Tissington Straits)

Lion Head Rock

Reynards Arch and Cave. Until her death in 1899, Sarah Gould of Mill Dale used to place a rope up to the arch every day in the hope of a tip.

Pickering Tor, where a lady once lived in the cave according to one old guide book!

Pickering Tor and the Watchbox. This group of tors is situated just downstream from Ilam Rock and on the Derbyshire bank. The Watchbox is the cube of rock on the top right hand corner of the rock face. In Victorian times it was supposed to be capable of being rocked

PICKERING TOR DOVE DALE 3930

Ilam Rock

Pickering Tor and Ilam Rock

The River Dove north of The Straits

The Watchbox, clearly visible in a precarious position at the top of the cliff face

Ilam Rock, looking upstream

The Ilam Rock refreshment room. This was situated where the footpath descends into the valley close to Ilam Rock. The photograph shows several tables and an awning for the visitors to sit under. Tea rooms seem to have been more popular in days gone by, but then planning permission was not a consideration!

The view from Dove Holes. There is much more scrub now compared to when this photograph was taken

The Church Rock, also recorded as the Captain's Rock on another photograph, opposite Doveholes

The valley upstream from Dove Holes

This intriguing photograph shows Viator Bridge at Mill Dale. Of special interest however is the end wall of Mill Dale mill. This mill was used during the nineteenth century as a colour mill. It ground iron ores from local mines to powder which was then used in whitewash to colour it red or yellow, depending on the ore used. Also of interest are the three walls running parallel to the bridge. Two may have been either side of the way into the mill. Was the nearest one to the bridge built as part of a sheep holding pen at dipping times?

There were several mills on the rivers Dove and Manifold. On the Dove, they were at Glutton, Crowdecote, Ludwell (north of Hartington), Hartington, Lode Mill (originally a lead smelting mill), Mill Dale, Thorpe, Okeover and at Hanging Bridge (Mayfield), plus others further downstream. On the Manifold, watermills existed at Longnor, (plus one about a ½ mile upstream), Ludburn, (strictly on the Black Brook), Brund, Westside and Wetton Mill.

The Okeover mill is mentioned in the Domesday Book. There was a medieval windmill at Sheen and a medieval watermill at Ilam. There were mills also at Warslow and Butterton on tributaries of the Manifold. Additionally there were waterwheels at the Dale lead mine (just above the Ecton to Warslow road); at the Ecton Mine lead slag mill which was served by a water supply from the Fishpond at East Ecton; at the Ecton Stamps Yard (a crushing mill, opposite Swainsley Hall) and at Botstone Mine, a half a mile upstream of Wetton Mill. Incidentally there was even a 33ft diameter water wheel erected in 1823 at river level deep inside the Ecton Mine and used for pumping

Pike Pool in Beresford Dale. There is still a footbridge where one can be seen in this view. The wall which today protects the Beresford estate near to the bridge had not been built

The fishing house of Charles Cotton and Izaak Walton on the Beresford estate. It was built in 1674. It is surrounded on three sides by the river

For many years a regular sight in the Beresford Dale area was Dora Oliver who acted as the water bailiff. The scourge of people who thought that the river was a playground, she was delightfully well informed and very popular. Here she is with the late Robert Thompson of Leek in about 1960. Her father had been the bailiff before her and she died on Christmas Eve, 1987

This fascinating photograph of Beresford Hall near Hartington, once the home of Charles Cotton, is probably the only one to survive. It was taken in 1857. It is described as 'The ruins of the West Wing'. In reality it was the intention of Mr Beresford-Hope, the owner to rebuild the house. However a shortage of funds stopped this. He rebuilt Sheen church and one to the same design in Maidstone, where he lived. After lying empty for years, the hall eventually became derelict and was demolished, perhaps as late as the 1880s. In the grounds there survive a prospect tower, rebuilt about a century ago, and Charles Cotton's fishing house. It originally had a bowling green in front of it plus huge trees which have subsequently been removed

The Charles Cotton Hotel at Hartington has been popular for over 100 years. These three photographs show early cars and a charabanc (an excursion by Porter & Co from Leek) outside the hotel

Two views of J M Nuttall's Hartington cheese factory, with various farmers unloading milk. By 1916, Mr Nuttall farmed 50 acres and also ran the cheese factory where 1.5 tons of cheese was made weekly, using the milk from nineteen farms. It started in the early 1870's using fifty gallons of milk per day, but was unused from 1894 to 1900 when Mr Nuttall acquired it and started making Stilton cheese

Another old industrial building in the village was the cotton mill, the large building on the right behind the Volunteers. It was built by Thomas Cantrell in 1776, but burnt down in 1786. In 1783, it employed sixty people. Opposite, some of the worker's cottages survive with the plaque 'T & JC 1777'. It records their construction by Thomas and Jane Cantrell. The old mill later became a penny lodging house. The Ashbourne Volunteers trained in Hartington every summer. The shop in the village (the large building on the left of the photograph) was also The Volunteer Arms but it lost its licence early in 1909. On the left is a view of the Corner House in the Market Place shown without any gardens and when it was two dwellings

The Market Place in Hartington

Hartington Dale, looking towards the village

The village pond or mere does not appear on a Hartington estate map of 1614 and presumably is more modern. Maybe the nearby 'Stanner' (an access to the old watercourse) is older. The pond was used to water livestock and fight fires in the days before the telephone, the nearest fire station being at Ashbourne. In the last 100 years or so, it has survived several calls for it to be filled in because it smelled badly and suffered from a lack of maintenance

Bassett's Garage and car showroom in the 1970's before it closed and was converted into the present Sheepskin and Tapestry shop

Photographed in Hartington Dale was this old character, fast asleep at the side of the road

The Friden Brickworks in 1950 with its siding adjacent to the Cromford and High Peak Railway (CHPR). Below is the Parsley Hay Station or Wharf, as it was known. The engine in the siding is standing where the cycle hire centre is now situated

Looking down the line towards Hartington Station at Parsley Hay in 1950 (above) and along the CHPR where it was crossed by the A515, also near Parsley Hay (below)

A number of photographs were taken at the beginning of this century in both Crowdecote and Longnor and used as postcards or lantern slides. They gave a fascinating insight into local rural life at the time. Here are two views of Mrs Horobin of Meadow Farm, Crowdecote. The view taken inside her house shows a typical locally made firegrate fitted into an existing fire surround

Two views of Crowdecote, one from the Longnor road and one from higher up on the ridge that runs down to Sheen

Two rare photographs of the ruins of Crowdecote Mill. It was situated down the lane opposite the entrance to the Packhorse Inn. It must have been to the left of the building visible in the previous two photographs, or did that building replace the old mill?

High Wheeldon, showing the north side from near Earl Sterndale. The postcard is dated 1928

Hollinsclough Chapel, built by John Lomas in his garden in 1801. He used to transport woven silk and silk-covered buttons by packhorse. The packhorse way in the middle of the photograph went to Gradbach silk mill and on to Macclesfield and its silk industry

Longnor used to be a busy community before motor transport brought Leek and Buxton so much nearer. Here are a series of scenes taken in the village. This shows a carrier in Carder Green near Sheffield House with the shops of a grocer and a corn dealer behind the cart and horse

A lovely view of the travelling shop near to the Market Place, taken outside the Horseshoe Inn

Izaak Smedley's cart, carrying passengers as well as goods from Longnor and photographed in Stockwell Street, Leek, presumably on market day

The village lockup was situated near the current fire station. Although now demolished, a further example may be seen at Alton in the Churnet Valley

Looking towards the Market Place with the smithy on the left (above)

Sam Sykes, the village cobbler. Note the glue pot on the shelf, the lockable drawer in the seat, a shoe horn above his head and clutter everywhere (below)

Mr George Tunnicliffe of Queen Street, setting off with his yoke to fetch water

Mary Ann was also recorded doing the same routine

Pitching hay into a barn at Hardingsbooth

Haymaking time at Longnor before the age of baling machines

Between Longnor and Hulme End is Brund Mill. It is situated on a packhorse road heading for Hartington and Pilsbury from Cheshire. This photo was taken around 1950

Fortunately a drawing of the old Brund packhorse bridge survives in 'Staffordshire Stiles and Derbyshire Dales', written by JP Sheldon who lived at Brund. It was published in 1894

Hulme End was the terminus of the Leek and Manifold Valley Light Railway, with the far end of the line at Waterhouses, where the narrow guage line met the standard guage line from Leek. The waiting room has recently been renovated. The coach shed on the right and the water tower have now gone but the engine shed (in the middle of the photograph) also survives

Three scenes in Warslow: The old post office (above) and Belfields shop on Cheadle road (middle). Note the milk churns on the right. It is possible that these were about to be delivered to the Ecton Creamery. The bottom photograph is of 'Landcroft', situated opposite the shop in the previous photograph

The Wooliscroft family outside the former Grouse Inn in Warslow. It closed around 1906-08 at a time when many small public or beer houses were shut for not meeting standards laid down under the Licensing Act, 1904. It had been the Temperance Hotel prior to opening as the Grouse Inn. The lower photograph shows the old inn

Ecton Mine in the mid 1880's. The current castle folly is on the site of the single storey house on the top left of the photo. The incline enabled tubs to be drawn up the hillside to the dressing floor where the ore was washed and crushed. None of the buildings shown here survive. The scene below, dating from 1883, shows the mine being prepared for reworking by Ecton Co Ltd, the last company to work the mine. The main mine entrance, Ecton Deep Level, can be seen although most activity took place in the Clayton Mine. The entrance to this can just be seen on the right

The Ecton Mine had an early Boulton and Watt winding engine housed in the building above. The roof has since been lowered because of high winds. The structure on the right is the remains of the chimney (above). During a drought in 1921 the Ecton creamery had insufficient water and installed this pump on the top of the drawing shaft in the Clayton Mine. This shaft is flooded and 960 feet deep. The photo was taken in 1924 (left)

Milk being unloaded at the Creamery at Ecton, established in eighteenth century mine buildings. The large building in the background was the Clock House smelter. It had a three feet diameter clock face on the north side of the building. The tank inscription (top left) reads 'United Dairies Creamery Ltd, Ecton'

The lower photograph shows the whole of the Creamery around 1930. Stone is being removed from the mine tips by both cart and lorry. There is a large infilled arch on the nearest building (the former south smelter). The area has the air of abandonment, despite deliveries of milk and daily collections by the train

An unusal view of the Ecton Mine and Creamery. Below the buildings is the entrance to the main Deep Ecton Adit, drilled in 1774. It intersected the drawing shaft, sunk at the side of the old engine house which can be seen at the top of the photograph (above left)

Richard Niness outside his home in Warslow. He was the manager of the Dale Lead Mine until it closed in 1873. The mine is situated just to the north of the Warslow to Ecton road. He later moved to Perry Dale, near Sparrowpit, where he became manager of the Peak Forest Mining Company (above right)

Staff at the Ecton Creamery. This closed in 1933 and the railway followed in 1934 (below)

Naylor's Temperance Hotel at Ecton Lea. These were quite popular in Victorian times. There was one in Warslow which became the Grouse Inn and another in Okeover, the current Okeover Arms. This was the era of the hydros in Buxton and Matlock where temperance was also practised. However it is held locally that while carrot juice was *de rigueur* in the hotel, gin was also available at the back door at Ecton Lea!

The Manifold train approaching Ecton Lea. To the right of the train are the navvies' huts where smallpox broke out in January 1903. There were two huts and one was empty. One navvy (John Graham, who slept in his own bed) went down with it and was taken to Bradley Wood Isolation Hospital near Ashbourne. He died shortly afterwards. There were five other beds in the same room, occupied by ten other navvies. Incredibly, the keeper of the hut and his family slept at the other end of the same hut. Two of the keeper's children and two other navvies also caught the disease and were sent to Bradley Wood. A year later, nine navvies working on the railway also caught smallpox and were sent to Bagnall Hospital near Stoke-on-Trent. However where they were billeted is not known

ECTON, MANIFOLD VALLEY.

The Cock Inn, Elkstones, when John Bradbury was the licensee. The girl with the yoke would be fetching water from the well opposite the pub and this was still in use in 1963 when the lower photograph was taken

Butterton ford in the early 1960's before the ford was concreted

Stamps's Bridge at Swainsley. It takes its name from the old mine stamps yard which was situated in the field below the bridge on the Ecton Hill side of the river. The mill was where the ore was crushed using a waterwheel. A tramway was laid from Ecton down the road to Swainsley to allow ore tubs to be pushed to the mill. It probably opened around 1818

An early view of Swainsley Hall, showing the original house built in 1864

Swainsley again, following extensions made in the 1890's

This view of Swainsley shows the final extension made in around 1910. Stamps bridge and Butterton Railway Station are visible in this scene

GAUNTS WOOD, MANIFOLD VALLEY.

Sir Thomas Wardle who lived at Swainsley Hall. Although a director of the Manifold Railway, he insisted on the building of a tunnel to protect his privacy. He was a friend of several of the Pre-Raphaelites and William Morris, Burne-Jones and their contemporaries were invited to stay at Swainsley Hall. He was a textile manufacturer at Leek, where his company, bearing his name, still survives. The photo below shows the construction of the north portal of Swainsley tunnel

Two views of Wetton Mill. ER Calthrop is shown here in the station. The platform was only six inches high (above). The station was opposite Dale Farm (below). Note the Sugar Loaf, a reef limestone knoll at the head of the valley behind the farm

Two views of Wetton Mill Farm and the valley train

ton Mill Station Manifold Valley North Stafford Railway.

The classic view of the train featured on postcards. It was clearly taken for publicity purposes as the train is empty and the crew (engine man, fireman and guard) are by the perimeter fence

The train passing Darfur Ridge at Wetton Mill, where the river disappears down a swallet hole in dry weather. There is now more scrub on the hillside beyond the train

MANIFOLD, VALLEY.

The protest meeting held at Wetton Mill in 1959 against the proposal to extend vehicular traffic down the old railway line from Redhurst Halt to Weags Bridge. This would have motorised the section between Swainsley tunnel and the Grindon — Wetton road (left)

Wetton Mill Bridge. It was built in 1807 after the previous bridge had been washed away. The stones across the river are the remains of the mill dam

Camping at Wetton Mill, Whitsuntide, 1963. Despite the obvious demand for a campsite here, it is no longer National Trust policy to permit it

The demolition train at Thor's Cave Station

Thor's Cave Station. The larger building was the refreshment room and the other building was the station waiting room. The latter were left standing at the stations when the line closed but suffered from vandalism and were eventually removed by the Staffordshire County Council

Grindon's pub, shown here as the Green Man Inn. The lane in the photograph is an old pack-horse way from Leek and Onecote to Alstonfield and Bakewell

Grindon village in 1903. Now the houses have been infilled with a terrace of council houses

Thor's Cave photographed about a century ago

Fetching water in Wetton. The building on the left is the pub

A view to Beeston Tor refreshment room, where the River Hamps meets the River Manifold. This hut, now disused, still survives. Beeston Tor has a cave, St Bertram's, where a hoard of Saxon coins and jewellery, including three gold rings and two silver brooches, were found in 1924. The coins were dated 871-874. Further coins were found and removed by lads from Grindon late one night while the excavation was taking place

Below Beeston Tor and high on the southern valley side is the ruined Throwley Hall. It dates from the early sixteenth century. The remains have been stabilised recently but it is a shame that it was allowed to decay to this state. Here and overleaf are three old views of the house

Throwley Hall

Throwley Hall

Down the river from Throwley lies Ilam, which has lost its hall, or at least the formal rooms. What remains was basically the servants' quarters. Fortunately some good photographs survive of the house. Here is the view from the river

The main floor was the middle of three floors visible in the main block on the photo. The oval shaped room with the three chimney stacks above was the Music Room. The windows to the right were part of the fifty feet long Drawing Room which occupied the corner of the house. The east front faced the church. The oval window on this side next to the Drawing Room was the library and the north east corner window was part of the Dining Room. The round structure on the roof was the top of the Lantern which contained the main staircase

A view of the Drawing Room looking towards the Music Room

Another view of the Drawing Room looking towards the Music Room

The hall became a hotel and the Drawing Room became the South Dining Room. Clearly it had been stripped of much of its finery and the outline of where the mirror over the fireplace used to be can just be seen

The Inner Hall, now the lower part of the Youth Hostel common room, although the floor has been raised. The photographer was standing in the outer hall which is the current Youth Hostel entrance hall and the bottom set of steps are behind its back wall

One of the old fireplaces together with a close up view of the columns (overleaf). This was sold to a film set when the hall was demolished

Demolition of the formal rooms took place in 1935. On the left of the top photo, the conservatory has almost gone. Underneath the balconied room was the Cabinet. It was fitted out with oak cabinets for displaying mineral specimens etc. To the right of this was the Music Room and then the Drawing Room

The lower photo shows the south wall of what is now the river side of the youth hostel. There were courtyards either side of the open doorway with the central portion of this photo being a passageway which went around two sides of the right hand courtyard to reach the formal rooms

Ilam church taken from the hall. The small trees on the edge of the churchyard are now fully grown and mask the view. In this photo, there is no boundary fence between the churchyard and the field

The interior of the church at the time the photo above was taken

This little bridge carried the footpath over the River Manifold from Paradise Walk towards Musden. A tree fell across it in the 1962 gale which did so much damage in the Peak and in Sheffield

A lovely view of the village before it was disfigured by the bus garage. The cottages near the hall were demolished and the village rebuilt here in the 1840's

The removal of the village meant that a new bridge had to be constructed across the River Manifold to replace St Bertram's bridge. It is a much larger structure than the single arched bridge it replaced

The cross of 1840 commemorates Mary Watts Russell, the daughter of David Pike Watts. Both father and daughter feature on the Chantrey carving in the church. The top of the cross came away in the 1962 gale. It is a poignant memorial, dating from 1826

A view of the cross and visitors to the village (above). The lower view may be of the hall staff

The mainstreet through Mappleton

The Okeover Temperance Hotel in 1936. It was situated in Mappleton but was on the Okeover Estate. It became licensed in 1964

The Manifold and the standard lines met at Waterhouses station. Here a North Stafford engine dwarfs the 30-inch guage Manifold engine

Three views around the area of the Green Man and Blacks Head Royal Hotel. Several of the properties have been demolished. The top right hand photo was taken prior to 1898 when the landlady, Mrs Fanny Wallis died

Midland 3F 0-6-0 Number 43402, photographed in September 1965 at Ashbourne. The station closed to all traffic on 1st June 1964

A local hunt meeting at the Newhaven Hotel

The elegant spire of St Oswalds. Ashbourne

The tollgate at Clifton near Ashbourne

An early view of Tissington Station